A MIND LIKE MINE

KEEP THE CONVERSATION GOING

This book looks at biographies of famous people from a diverse range of backgrounds and lots of big themes, which could leave you feeling emotional yourself. We encourage you to read this book with an open mind and talk to friends, family, and trusted adults about what you've learned and how it has made you feel.

WIDE EYED EDITIONS

Dear Reader,

I have a smile on my face as I write this note, because if you're reading this, it means **YOU ARE ABOUT TO DISCOVER SOMETHING THAT TOOK ME DECADES TO FIND OUT.** When I was growing up, no one really talked to me about mental health, and I didn't understand too much about it. As a young adult, I started experiencing periods of severe anxiety and depression.

When I was first diagnosed with mental health disorders, I felt lost and isolated, **DESPITE THE SUPPORT OF FRIENDS AND FAMILY.** I realized I had no role models who had openly discussed their mental health, so I started researching. To my surprise, **I DISCOVERED THAT MANY OF THE GREATEST MINDS THROUGHOUT HISTORY HAD LIVED WITH MENTAL HEALTH DISORDERS.** I remember feeling a huge sense of relief, that it wasn't just me going through this, and that having a mental health condition did not need to stop me from fulfilling my dreams. It is what inspired me to write this book.

So, what are you about to learn that I wish I'd known when I was younger? First and foremost, that **WE ARE ALL IN THIS TOGETHER.** Not everyone lives with a mental health disorder, but we all have mental health, and it shouldn't be a secret! **TALKING OPENLY ABOUT OUR EMOTIONAL EXPERIENCES HELPS US ALL TO BETTER UNDERSTAND OURSELVES AND EACH OTHER.** It's important to use appropriate language when talking about mental health and differentiate stigma from the truth. This book is proof that not only has our medical understanding and treatments for mental health disorders improved dramatically over the centuries, but also so has our empathy for one another. In every corner of greatness, from groundbreaking scientists to sporting legends and musicians, people living with mental health disorders have excelled in their passions and shown that **ANYTHING IS POSSIBLE WHEN YOU PUT YOUR MIND TO IT.**

Rachael x

Foreword

When my son began showing symptoms of anxiety and depression at a young age, **I FELT COMPLETELY OVERWHELMED.** The deafening silence around children's mental health at that time meant **IT FELT IMPOSSIBLE TO FIND THE HELP AND RESOURCES WE NEEDED.** My son was ten years old when he was hospitalized and diagnosed with bipolar disorder and I was desperate to support his recovery. I wanted him to know that **HE WAS NOT ALONE.** While I was comforted to learn that mental health disorders are common, treatable, and can often begin early in life, I was astounded I had been completely in the dark about this before my son's diagnosis.

As I learned more about mental health disorders and how society may affect why we don't access treatment earlier, it became my mission to change the narrative around mental health and improve mental health literacy. **NO FAMILY SHOULD HAVE TO NAVIGATE CARING FOR THEIR CHILDREN'S MENTAL HEALTH WITHOUT SUPPORT.** In 2016, I founded The Youth Mental Health Project, in the USA. This is a nonprofit organization that seeks to educate, support, and empower families and communities to better understand and care for the mental health of young people.

I am so proud that The Youth Mental Health Project is endorsing this illuminating book and cannot thank the author enough for writing it! Rachael brilliantly weaves together the true stories of famous people who have lived with various mental health disorders with easy-to-follow explanations of common mental health conditions. *A Mind Like Mine* is the perfect book for those who want to learn more while being inspired by people who have **ACHIEVED GREATNESS WHILE LIVING WITH MENTAL HEALTH DISORDERS.**

Randi Silverman

Founder of The Youth Mental Health Project

Michelangelo

(1475-1564)

Born in 15th-century Caprese in Italy, Michelangelo is one of the greatest artists who has ever lived. Michelangelo became so famous for his sculptures and frescoes that two biographies of him were written while he was still alive. It is from these accounts, alongside his letters, that we can discover more about his temperament, behavior, and health.

Becoming an artist was looked down upon for a man in a noble family like Michelangelo's. Nevertheless, when Michelangelo was 14 he pursued his passion for his art and became an artist apprentice in Florence. Afterwards, he traveled to Bologna and then Rome where he completed his famous sculpture *Pietà* in 1496. Five years later, his status as a major artist was established when he was commissioned to sculpt *David* for the cathedral of Florence. After it was finished, he traveled to Rome at the request of Pope Julius II, and created his iconic frescoes on the ceiling of the Sistine Chapel in the Vatican. But despite his enviable success as an artist, Michelangelo's letters reveal that through these years he often felt unhappy.

Michelangelo experienced periods of melancholy (a pensive sadness and gloomy state of mind) throughout his life. His first biographers both highlight that he had difficulties sleeping and often lost his appetite. This has led some people to believe that Michelangelo likely lived with depression. He has also been described by some as a perfectionist with a temper who became obsessed with his work and often wanted to be alone. Michelangelo's obsessive nature has led some people to assume that he lived with obsessive-compulsive disorder (OCD). However, retrospective diagnoses are notoriously difficult. Some scholars have explained that Michelangelo's intense focus (or obsession) on his artistic projects more closely resembles traits of autism, rather than an obsessive compulsion that would be more consistent with OCD. Back in the 16th century, conditions such as clinical depression, OCD, and autism were not yet known and so there are no definitive records to confirm Michelangelo's suspected conditions.

Our understanding of mental health disorders and neurodiversity has improved dramatically since the days of Michelangelo, as have the medical and social support available. In a letter in 1524, Michelangelo spoke about how he was treated by those around him: "YET BECAUSE THEY SAY THEY FIND ME IN SOME WAY STRANGE AND OBSESSED, WHICH HARMS NO ONE BUT MYSELF, THEY PRESUME TO SPEAK ILL OF ME AND TO ABUSE ME."

In the later years of Michelangelo's life, his artistic endeavors focussed more heavily on poetry and architectural projects such as the church of St Peter. Today, people continue to travel from all over the world to marvel at Michelangelo's artistic accomplishments.

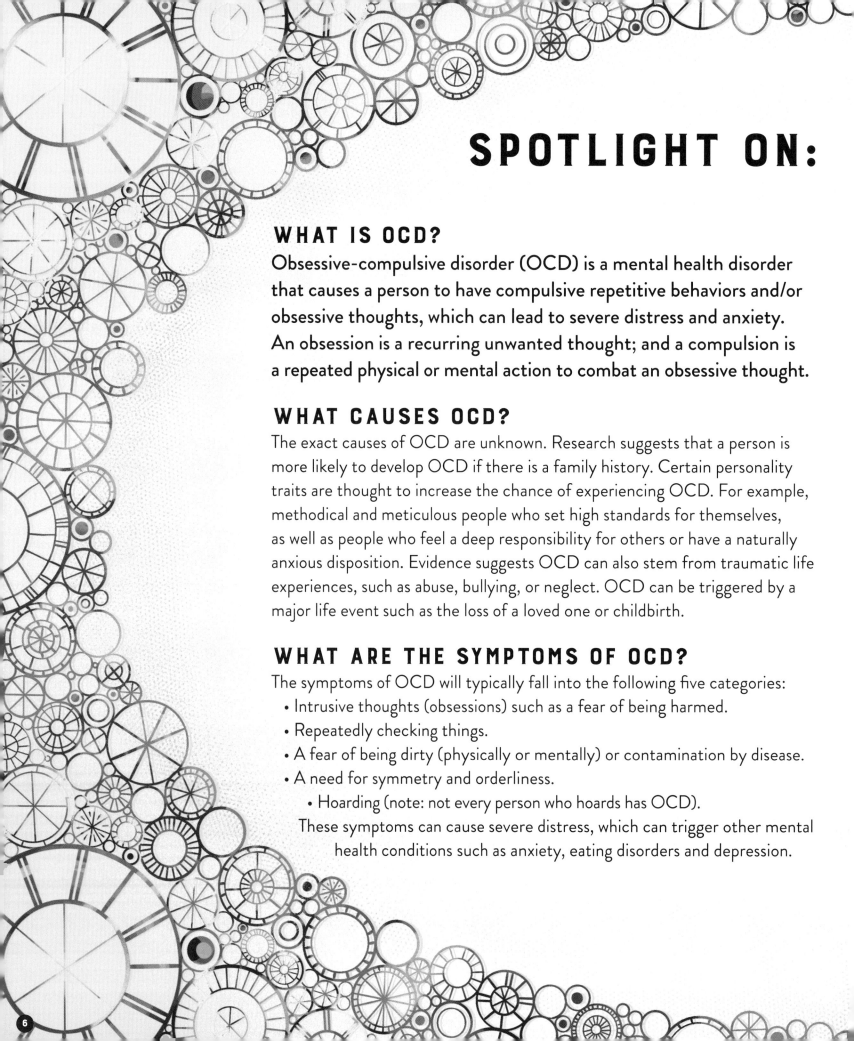

SPOTLIGHT ON:

WHAT IS OCD?

Obsessive-compulsive disorder (OCD) is a mental health disorder that causes a person to have compulsive repetitive behaviors and/or obsessive thoughts, which can lead to severe distress and anxiety. An obsession is a recurring unwanted thought; and a compulsion is a repeated physical or mental action to combat an obsessive thought.

WHAT CAUSES OCD?

The exact causes of OCD are unknown. Research suggests that a person is more likely to develop OCD if there is a family history. Certain personality traits are thought to increase the chance of experiencing OCD. For example, methodical and meticulous people who set high standards for themselves, as well as people who feel a deep responsibility for others or have a naturally anxious disposition. Evidence suggests OCD can also stem from traumatic life experiences, such as abuse, bullying, or neglect. OCD can be triggered by a major life event such as the loss of a loved one or childbirth.

WHAT ARE THE SYMPTOMS OF OCD?

The symptoms of OCD will typically fall into the following five categories:
- Intrusive thoughts (obsessions) such as a fear of being harmed.
- Repeatedly checking things.
- A fear of being dirty (physically or mentally) or contamination by disease.
- A need for symmetry and orderliness.
- Hoarding (note: not every person who hoards has OCD).

These symptoms can cause severe distress, which can trigger other mental health conditions such as anxiety, eating disorders and depression.

OBSESSIVE-COMPULSIVE DISORDER (OCD)

OCD VS AUTISM

Repetitive behavioral patterns can be common in autistic people, but OCD and repetitive behaviors in autism should not be confused.

Unlike OCD, autism is not a mental health disorder—it is a lifelong neurodevelopmental disorder. It is a spectrum condition, meaning that it will have a different level and type of impact on each person. Due to our mainly neurotypical society, autistic people present with a range of behavioral challenges: social interaction and communication difficulties, over- or under-sensitivity to the senses, emotional meltdowns, intense interests in hobbies, and repetitive behaviors. In many cases, an autistic person will also experience mental health disorders such as anxiety, depression, and sometimes OCD.

For an autistic person, repetitive and restrictive behaviors can be enjoyable and a comfort. But a person living with OCD tends to find the repetitive and restrictive behaviors distressing and detrimental to their daily activities. For example, an autistic person may wash their hands repetitively and enjoy how it feels, while a non-autistic person living with OCD may wash their hands repetitively because they have an obsessive thought that if they don't do it, something bad will happen. Because some autistic traits appear to mirror the symptoms of obsessive-compulsive disorder, OCD can sometimes go undiagnosed in autistic people.

SIR ISAAC NEWTON

(1643-1727)

Born in Lincolnshire, England, Sir Isaac Newton paved the way for modern technology through his discoveries in optics, mathematics, and physics. Isaac lived a life of three parts: he had a lonely childhood, followed by an extraordinary scientific career, and, finally, after experiencing a period of emotional distress, he began the third chapter of his life as a civil servant.

Isaac never knew his father, who died before he was born. When Isaac was three, his mother remarried and went to live with her new husband, leaving Isaac to be raised by his grandmother until he was ten. His childhood appears to have been incredibly lonely and he didn't have many friends as an adult either. Some scholars believe these feelings of loneliness and separation from his mother as a child may have caused trauma that impacted Isaac's mental health in later life.

After attending a local grammar school, Isaac went to study at the University of Cambridge in 1661. When the plague swept through Cambridge, Isaac returned home to the country to escape the deadly disease. Continuing his studies at home by himself, Isaac mastered mathematics. He returned to Cambridge in 1667 and two years later, having impressed his colleagues with his genius, he was appointed as a professor—just eight years after first attending university.

Isaac devoted 27 more years to science. In 1692, Isaac quite unexpectedly experienced a dramatic change in his mental health, marked by the sudden onset of psychosis. Isaac stopped eating and sleeping. He became depressed and after experiencing delusions that his friends were against him, he isolated himself from everyone. But as quickly as his symptoms appeared, they passed 18 months later seemingly on their own. He got back in touch with his friends to explain his behavior: **"I… HAVE NEITHER ATE NOR SLEPT WELL THIS TWELVE MONTH, NOR HAVE I MY FORMER CONSISTENCY OF MIND."**

What caused this fluctuation in Isaac's mental health is highly debated by scholars. Some argue that it was the result of mercury poisoning caused by his scientific experiments. However, other scholars have discounted this theory, because Isaac did not appear to have the physical symptoms of mercury poisoning, and instead have retrospectively diagnosed Isaac with depression.

Isaac's recovery marked a turning point in his life. In 1696, Isaac left Cambridge and his career in science behind. He was appointed Warden and then Master of the Royal Mint, working as a civil servant for the last 30 years of his life. Isaac excelled in his new career, and in 1705 was knighted by the queen. Isaac achieved greatness in not one but two completely different careers and his work changed the world forever.

HANS CHRISTIAN ANDERSEN

(1805–1875)

Danish author Hans Christian Andersen created many of the world's most iconic fairy tales including *The Ugly Duckling*, *The Little Mermaid*, *The Emperor's New Clothes*, and *Thumbelina*. These stories have been retold and reimagined over time. Hans' original tales often included darker endings with themes of sorrow, inspired by his own feelings of loneliness and depression.

Growing up in a low-income family in Odense, Hans dreamed of becoming an actor. His lack of education prevented this at the time, but with support from the Director of the Royal Theatre, Jonas Collin, Hans attended a grammar school in Slagelse at the age of 17. Mocked for being older than the other children, it was a lonely and unhappy time. Hans began lodging with the headmaster Simon Meisling, who treated Hans so unkindly that he fell into a depression. In 1825, Hans began to keep a diary, which allowed him to express his feelings. In an early entry, he wrote: **"DEPRESSION, A NASTY DOWNPOUR, GREY AND AUTUMN-LIKE OUTSIDE, FOGGY AND RAW, AS IN MY SOUL."**

Hearing of Hans' distress, Jonas moved him to Copenhagen in 1827 to continue his studies. Hans was much happier in his new home, which was a short walk from the harbor that features in *The Little Mermaid*. In 1828, Hans went to study at the University of Copenhagen. During his time at university, he self-published a fantastical tale. It became an instant success and was the start of Hans' prolific career as a writer.

Soon after, Hans fell in love with a girl named Riborg. When she married someone else, Hans slipped into another period of depression. This was the first of many unrequited love interests in Hans' life, with people of different genders. Throughout his life, Hans felt lonely and struggled to make many friends. His humble beginnings led many to see him as a social climber. Hans felt like an outsider, never fully accepted.

Hans' first book of fairy tales, which included classic stories such as *The Princess and the Pea,* was published in 1835. His style of storytelling broke away from literary traditions, combining folk legends with autobiographical elements and big emotional themes, something that many authors at the time didn't do. While he wrote stories for children, he always kept the adult reader in mind.

A few years later, Hans began receiving money from the government, which gave him the financial stability to continue writing. But, despite his growing literary reputation, Hans continued to feel incredibly lonely and experienced bouts of depression for the rest of his life. After his death, Hans' fairy tales continued to grow in popularity and today are considered classics. Hans saw himself as the ugly duckling: an awkward outsider, who—through the power of his storytelling—became a swan.

SPOTLIGHT ON: DEPRESSION

WHAT IS DEPRESSION?

Depression is the persistent feeling of sadness that lasts for a prolonged period. It is often misunderstood and seen as a sign of weakness, but it is not. Depression can significantly impact a person's everyday life.

WHAT CAUSES DEPRESSION?

Depression can be triggered by lots of things including big life events, such as the death of a loved one, or bullying. It can also be caused by loneliness or the stress of living with a life-threatening illness, such as cancer. There are many different forms of depression, including postnatal depression that can be experienced after the birth of a child. However, there is not always an obvious cause of depression. People with a family history of depression are more likely to experience depression in their lifetime.

WHAT ARE THE SYMPTOMS OF DEPRESSION?

Depression impacts people in different ways. The most common symptoms of depression are feelings of emptiness, sadness, hopelessness, and low self-esteem. Often, people experience a loss of interest in things they would usually enjoy and may feel tearful, guilt-ridden, irritable, or moody. These feelings might make a person avoid seeing family and friends. Physical symptoms may include tiredness, aches, and pains, and routine tasks such as getting dressed and making decisions may feel much harder. Some may experience a loss of appetite, while others may over-eat. Severe depression can cause thoughts of self-harm or suicide.

A COMMON MISCONCEPTION

Depression is not something a person can "snap out of." However, it is treatable. Many people make a full recovery without any relapses, but others may live with a degree of depression throughout their lives.

SPOTLIGHT ON: TALKING ABOUT MENTAL HEALTH

The language we use to describe our mental health, and the mental health of others, plays a vital role in breaking down some of the misconceptions and stigmas that surround emotional wellbeing. This is an ever-evolving conversation. Being open-minded, empathic, and thoughtful in language choices can make a huge difference to society.

Today, words such as "crazy" and "mad" remain a problematic and inaccurate stereotype when discussing an individual living with mental health conditions. Using words that are diagnostic in nature, such as "bipolar" or "OCD," as adjectives in general conversations sensationalizes the truth and contributes to mental health stigma. For example, sometimes a person who does not experience OCD, will describe an action or certain behavior as proof "I'm so OCD." This can be harmful to people who live with OCD as it can lead to an inaccurate understanding of the condition.

Word choices matter, so it's important to use language that emphasizes the person rather than their mental health condition or disorder.

PHRASES TO USE	PHRASES TO AVOID
Mental health conditions/disorders	Mental illness
People with mental health conditions/disorders	"Mentally ill people"/"mental patient"/"crazy people"/"lunatic"/"nutjob"/"psycho"
They live with [a mental health condition] They are being treated for [a mental health disorder]	They are "a victim of"/"suffering from"/"afflicted with"/"struggling from"/"crippled by"
They live with bipolar disorder/OCD/schizophrenia	They are bipolar/OCD/schizophrenic
Died by suicide	Committed suicide
Their behavior was unusual or out of character	They were acting "crazy"/"deranged"/"mad"/"psychotic"

Charles Darwin

(1809-1882)

Charles Darwin's theory of natural selection shook the world of science and religion, forever changing how we understand the theory of evolution. He spent over two decades gathering evidence to convince his fellow scientists about his groundbreaking scientific discovery. What makes this achievement even more remarkable is that he did it while living with anxiety and chronic pain from an undiagnosed illness.

Born in Shrewsbury, England, Charles was encouraged by his father to become a doctor. When that didn't work out, his father suggested he led a religious life. But in 1831, Charles received an unexpected invitation to be Captain Fitzroy's companion aboard a ship called the HMS *Beagle*. He felt a swirl of emotions. Although he was excited to go on an adventure, Charles was gripped by a deep sadness at the thought of having to be away from his family for so long. He later revealed in his autobiography that he had been experiencing heart palpitations at this time but sought no treatment, afraid that doctors would advise against the trip.

Instead, Charles set sail on a voyage that would last almost five years. He explored South America and the Galapagos islands, surveying plants and animals and classifying all the new species he found. While observing fossils, Charlies realized that the animals' features varied over time and by region. Had they adapted to increase their chance of survival? Slowly, the theory of natural selection began to form in his mind. Charles sent samples of his discoveries to England—he was becoming quite the celebrity back home. But life was not all smooth sailing for Charles when he returned to England.

Charles quickly discovered that fame had a negative affect on his health. Just a few minutes addressing his peers at a scientific meeting could bring on 24 hours of vomiting. From then on, for the sake of his health, Charles avoided social gatherings and he moved to the country with his wife, Emma. For the rest of his life, when Emma was away, Charles experienced a multitude of physical symptoms including vomiting, heart palpitations, shivering, hysterical bouts of crying, fainting, nervousness, and a feeling that he might die. This has led some historians and healthcare professionals to suggest Charles lived with panic disorder and agoraphobia (avoiding situations that may cause anxiety).

Despite the best efforts of doctors at the time, Charles' health significantly impacted the way he lived. Yet his passion for the natural world never wavered. His solitude allowed him to focus on his scientific work and Charles finally presented his theory in his book, *On the Origin of Species*, in 1859.

"EVEN ILL-HEALTH, THOUGH IT HAS ANNIHILATED SEVERAL YEARS OF MY LIFE, HAS SAVED ME FROM THE DISTRACTIONS OF SOCIETY AND AMUSEMENT."

ADA LOVELACE

(1815-1852)

Born in England, Ada Lovelace was a pioneer of computer programming. Ada experienced many illnesses throughout her life, both physical and mental. Despite her health conditions, Ada was determined to pursue her passion for mathematics.

Ada was the daughter of Lady Byron, whose own keen interest in mathematics led to her being nicknamed "the princess of parallelograms," and Romantic poet, Lord Byron. She was just a baby when her father left the country, never to return. Historians believe that Lord Byron may have lived with bipolar disorder and the condition appears to have run in the family, as Ada too displayed symptoms of the condition later in life. Ada was raised by her mother, who educated her in a range of subjects.

When Ada was seven, she developed severe headaches that impacted her eyesight and ability to read. Later, when she was 13, she caught measles, which left her bedridden for several years, only able to sit up for an hour a day. When she was strong enough, she continued her studies in bed. She slowly regained the use of her legs and by the age of 17 she was able to walk and be introduced into society, as was the custom of the time. Around this time she met Charles Babbage and became fascinated by his "Analytical Engine," which was an early type of computer. Babbage became one of several mathematical friends and mentors to Ada, later nicknaming her the "Enchantress of Numbers."

Two years later, in 1835, Ada married Lord King who became the Earl of Lovelace and the couple had three children together. Despite the 19th-century expectations on Ada as a wife and mother, she continued to study mathematics. In 1843, aged 27, Ada published a translated mathematical paper alongside her own "Notes" on Babbage's Analytical Engine, which presented the first computer program as well as her own commentary on the creative potential of the machine. While Babbage had thought of his Analytical Engine like a calculator, Ada had the vision to see its potential was much greater.

Throughout her adult life, Ada wrote letters describing depressive episodes alongside periods of mania, which has led some scholars today to retrospectively diagnose Ada with bipolar disorder. However, given Ada's history of physical illnesses and the range of treatments she had, we can't know for certain. Yet another illness saw her brilliant life come to an end all too early when she died at the age of 36 from cervical cancer. In 1992, a commemorative plaque was placed on Ada's former home. It reads, "Pioneer of Computing lived here."

Florence Nightingale

(1820-1910)

Known as the "Lady of the Lamp" from her time working as a trauma nurse in the Crimean War, Florence Nightingale revolutionized the profession of nursing. After the war, Florence carried out the majority of her reform campaigning from her bedside, due to her health. Her symptoms led some scholars to suspect that she had Crimean fever and may also have lived with bipolar disorder and post-traumatic stress disorder (PTSD).

Florence was deeply religious and felt that nursing was her calling from God. Breaking from the societal expectations of a 19th-century middle-class woman, she trained as a nurse. In 1854, Florence led a team of 38 nurses in a military hospital in Turkey to help injured soldiers in the Crimean War. She ensured good levels of hygiene to aid the soldiers' physical recovery and also prioritized their mental wellbeing, helping them write letters home to their families. Florence recognized the impact of anxiety on a person's overall health: **"APPREHENSION, UNCERTAINTY, WAITING, EXPECTATION, FEAR OF SURPRISE, DO A PATIENT MORE HARM THAN ANY EXERTION."**

Florence's unprecedented levels of care reduced the mortality rate of the injured soldiers. She traveled from Turkey to Crimea and shortly afterwards fell ill. Nevertheless, she refused to return to England until the last soldiers returned in 1856. For almost 30 years after returning from the Crimean War, Florence experienced a range of debilitating symptoms that kept her from leaving the house, including intermittent fever, loss of appetite, fatigue, insomnia, irritability, depression, sciatica, shortness of breath, and palpitations.

It is widely believed by scholars today that Florence had a bacterial infection known as brucellosis (or Crimean fever) but in addition to this, it has been suggested that she may also have been living with mental health conditions such as bipolar disorder and PTSD. One theory is that Florence experienced PTSD as a result of her time spent treating people injured in the war. We cannot know for sure—there is no record of her experiencing symptoms such as flashbacks or nightmares. However, after she returned home from the war, she did isolate herself and never treated the sick again, which could have been a way to avoid triggering the painful memories.

While we will never know for certain what conditions Florence lived with, we do know that even in her hardest, bedridden times she never gave up fighting to improve healthcare standards, from ward designs to hygiene and recovery processes. She also wrote over 200 books and reports on healthcare, and thousands of letters to influential people, including Queen Victoria, in her campaign to change the healthcare system. In 1860, Florence set up the Nightingale Training School for nurses. Today, the International Day of Nursing is celebrated every year on the anniversary of Florence's birth, 12 May.

SPOTLIGHT ON: PTSD

WHAT IS PTSD?

Post-traumatic stress disorder (PTSD) is a mental health disorder that causes distress for a person who has been exposed to a traumatic event or series of events. It is natural for someone to feel a range of emotions following a dangerous or frightening event. However, some people develop symptoms that seriously impact their lives, for a prolonged period of time, and may be diagnosed with PTSD. Often PTSD develops within three months of a traumatic event, but sometimes it can begin years later. Recovery time varies for each individual, and it is possible for PTSD to be treated many years after the trauma, so it is never too late to seek help.

WHAT CAUSES PTSD?

There are many types of severe trauma that can trigger PTSD. Some are one-off events, such as a serious accident or childbirth, while other traumas may take place over an extended period of time, such as physical assault or abuse, violence or neglect as well as severe physical illnesses, living through a war, or torture. PTSD tends to be more severe if the trauma occurs in childhood and/or is caused by a parent or guardian. It can also be more severe if the person was alone when they experienced the trauma, or they remain in contact with the person who caused the trauma. It is not known why some people develop PTSD and others do not. One theory is that PTSD is a survival mechanism to help prepare an individual to survive future trauma. Some studies suggest PTSD could be the result of increased levels of stress hormones such as adrenaline or variations in how the brain processes emotions. People who have lived with depression or anxiety are more likely to develop PTSD if they experience a severe trauma.

WHAT ARE THE SYMPTOMS OF PTSD?

One of the most common symptoms of PTSD is reliving or re-experiencing the severe trauma in the person's mind. This may be through dreams, involuntary memories, or flashbacks. Someone with PTSD may begin to obsess over the event, asking "what-if" type questions. Symptoms can also be physical in nature, such as sweating, pain, shaking, and feeling sick. Difficulty sleeping and concentrating are also symptoms. A person experiencing PTSD may experience hyperarousal and anxiety, making them irritable and prone to angry outbursts. They may go to extreme lengths to try to avoid reminders of the event and may try to distract themselves through other activities or become very isolated and withdrawn. They may experience changes in their mood, including a loss of interest in activities they previously found enjoyable, feelings of negativity, guilt or blame, and sometimes have trouble with memory. In cases of severe PTSD, a person may also have symptoms of self-harm, alcohol misuse, drug misuse, and suicidal thoughts.

SECONDARY TRAUMA

Secondary trauma occurs when an individual hears a firsthand account of another person's traumatic experience. This indirect exposure to a traumatic event or series of events can led to a person developing PTSD, which some people refer to as "secondary PTSD." The group of people most at risk of secondary PTSD are medical healthcare professionals and charity workers who spend a significant amount of time listening to people talk in-depth about their traumatic experiences. Therapists are trained to do this, however, in some cases, it can lead to the healthcare professional themselves experiencing symptoms of PTSD. It is therefore important that healthcare professionals are aware of their own mental wellbeing, and practice self-care.

ALFRED NOBEL

(1833-1896)

Born in Stockholm, Sweden, Alfred left two everlasting impacts on the world: dynamite and the Nobel Prizes. Alongside his scientific work, Alfred was a prolific writer. From his letters, historians and researchers have been able to gain some understanding about his physical and mental wellbeing. Throughout his life, Alfred experienced several bouts of depression.

Alfred came from a long line of inventors and engineers. As a young boy, he and his family moved to St Petersburg in Russia where his father had a successful mechanical workshop, creating sea mines during the Crimean War. After the war, business dried up so the family moved back to Sweden where Alfred began experimenting with nitroglycerine to make explosives. Some of his experiments went wrong and people were killed, including his younger brother Emil in 1864. The government banned experiments in Stockholm, but neither this nor his brother's death deterred Alfred. He began experimenting outside the capital and discovered that by mixing nitroglycerine with sand called "kieselguhr," he could create a powerful explosive which he named "dynamite."

Dynamite revolutionized the mining and construction industries. Alfred had hoped that dynamite might put an end to war, but instead it was weaponized and cost millions of people their lives. Alfred never married or had children and in his will he left the majority of his fortune to found the Nobel Prizes, including the Nobel Peace Prize. Alfred was very dedicated to his work, but he did find it lonely at times, and often wrote in his letters that he felt depressed. Alongside his scientific work, he also wrote novels, plays, poems, and pithy statements on life known as aphorisms. For example, Alfred wrote: **"WORRY IS THE STOMACH'S WORST POISON."**

Alfred also had to contend with many physical health problems. He frequently had indigestion, severe headaches, and towards the end of his life he developed angina (chest pain). In a letter in 1888, he wrote: **"FOR SOME TIME I HAVE BEEN SICK AND DEPRESSED. THIS IS WHAT HAPPENS EACH TIME I OVEREXERT MYSELF. BUT WHAT CAN I DO?"**

Alfred died in 1896 in San Remo, Italy. The first Nobel Prizes were awarded in 1901. It is speculated that Alfred included a prize for Physiology or Medicine because of his own experience with poor physical health and depression. However, to date, very few Nobel Prizes have been awarded for psychiatry. In 1949, Antonio Egas Moniz won for showing a leucotomy could "mitigate severe symptoms of serious mental illnesses." However, this theory has since been disproven. As the world begins to acknowledge the importance of mental health, we can only hope that more Nobel Prizes will be awarded for advances in psychiatry in the future.

VINCENT VAN GOGH

(1853-1890)

Vincent Van Gogh was one of the greatest artists who ever lived, producing more than 850 paintings and 1,300 works on paper in just ten years. He famously cut off his left ear, but what is less well-known is Vincent's mental health leading up to and after the incident.

Growing up in Zundert in the Netherlands, Vincent didn't find school easy and never finished. He tried many different jobs after leaving school, but it wasn't until he was 27 that he turned his focus to art, when his brother Theo suggested it. The two brothers were very close and Theo supported Vincent financially throughout his life. Vincent studied painting in The Hague with his uncle, Anton Mauve, before moving to Paris where he was influenced by Impressionist artists such as Claude Monet. Vincent began to use bright colors and short brush strokes in his paintings, creating his own iconic style. But Vincent soon tired of the busyness of Paris and he rented four rooms in a yellow house in Arles in the South of France. He hoped other artists would join him to make his artist-life less lonely.

Vincent's friend Paul Gauguin joined him, but their personalities clashed and they had heated arguments over creative differences. Vincent became increasingly agitated and on 23 December 1888, Paul decided to leave. Vincent was so upset that he threatened Paul with a razor. Later that same day, Vincent cut off his left ear. Theo rushed to the hospital and discovered Vincent had hardly any memory of what had happened. Five months later, Vincent admitted himself to the Saint-Paul-de-Mausole psychiatric hospital in Saint-Rémy where he hoped his mental health would improve. In a letter to Theo, Vincent referred to his mental health condition as "madness," a term that we no longer use to describe mental health conditions today. He wrote: **"I'M BEGINNING TO CONSIDER [A MENTAL ILLNESS] AS AN ILLNESS LIKE ANY OTHER."**

There was little understanding of mental health conditions in the 19th century and so the exact mental health disorders Vincent lived with are unknown. Historians and medical professionals have attempted to diagnose Vincent retrospectively, and many believe he was living with bipolar disorder. Vincent was released from the hospital in May 1890. His health seemed to be improving, but a change in Theo's financial circumstances weighed on Vincent's mind. Vincent died by suicide on 29 July 1890 and is now buried next to his brother Theo in Auvers-sur-Oise.

Although Vincent lived less than two years after his most famous episode of psychosis, in that time he produced some of his most acclaimed works, including *Starry Night* and *Almond Blossom*. Many of these works were scenes he observed from his bedroom window in the Saint Paul psychiatric hospital and on nature walks.

NIKOLA TESLA

(1856-1943)

Considered the "quintessential mad scientist," Serbian-American inventor Nikola Tesla was undoubtedly treated differently to his scientific peers because of his eccentricities and bold scientific claims. Even as a child, Nikola loved inventing things, but after the death of his "genius" older brother, Nikola developed low self-esteem: **"ANYTHING I DID THAT WAS CREDITABLE MERELY CAUSED MY PARENTS TO FEEL THEIR LOSS MORE KEENLY. SO I GREW UP WITH LITTLE CONFIDENCE IN MYSELF."**

In 1875, Nikola studied Engineering at the Polytechnic in Graz. One of his lectures sparked the idea of harnessing alternating current (AC). Over the next decade, Nikola spent time working and studying in Europe before moving to America in 1884. Nikola became a contemporary and rival of Thomas Edison, via "The War of the Currents." While Edison invented the light bulb using direct current (DC), it is Nikola's AC that powers the world. AC is used in electric cars such as those made by Elon Musk, who named his company "Tesla" after Nikola.

Despite his accomplishments, Nikola struggled to get funding to develop his later projects because his peers began to think his ideas were "crazy." Nikola claimed to have invented an "earthquake machine" that could crumble a building in minutes, as well as a "death ray" that could destroy aircrafts. Furthermore, Nikola is said to have displayed a range of compulsive behaviors and phobias. He could not stand jewelery and was fascinated by the number three and its multiples. He spent the final years of his life living on the 33rd floor of the New Yorker Hotel in apartment number 3327 and reportedly walked around buildings three times before entering. Some scholars today believe Nikola's repetitive behaviors indicate that he lived with obsessive-compulsive disorder (OCD). However, retrospective diagnoses are always open to interpretation. Some believe Nikola was autistic, while others have linked his obsessions with pigeons and cleanliness to contracting cholera from dirty drinking water or the loss of his brother.

Sadly, mental health disorders and neurodiversity were not understood at that time. Even in the 21st century, words such as "crazy" and "mad" remain a problematic and inaccurate stereotype when discussing someone living with mental health conditions. Nikola was isolated from the conventional science community in his final years and died penniless. Despite his peers considering his scientific ideas preposterous, the US government seized all of Nikola's papers after he died. Indeed, many current scholars believe Nikola's scientific views were simply ahead of their time. Nikola's work has led to many technological advancements, including wireless communications, lasers, lighting, radar, and robotics.

Marie Curie

(1867-1934)

Polish-born scientist Marie Curie was the first woman to earn a doctorate in France. She went on to become the first woman to win a Nobel Prize, and the first person ever to win two Nobel Prizes. She was also the first female scientist to be targeted by a smear campaign that would severely impact her mental health.

Growing up in Warsaw, Marie's career in science didn't always look certain. When her father fell into financial difficulties, Marie came up with a plan to work as a governess to fund her sister through medical school and then in return, her sister would one day support her studies. It was a brilliant plan, but the reality was tough. In her letters, Marie often spoke of feeling melancholy as her dreams of studying science felt unreachable. She once wrote to her sister, "TODAY I AM EXCEPTIONALLY UNHAPPY IN THIS WORLD. THINK OF ME WITH TENDERNESS—PERHAPS I SHALL BE ABLE TO FEEL IT EVEN HERE."

When her sister was able to offer her lodgings in Paris, Marie's dreams got back on track and she began studying Physics and Mathematics at Sorbonne University, aged 24. In 1894, Marie met fellow scientist and her future husband, Pierre Curie. After giving birth to their first child, Irene, Marie was soon back in the laboratory working with Pierre. Their research on radiation earned them the Nobel Prize in Physics in 1903.

In 1906, when their second child, Eve, was just a toddler, tragedy struck the Curie family when Pierre was killed in a horse and carriage accident. Marie was devastated. Now a single mother to two young children, Marie threw herself into her scientific work, continuing Pierre's scientific endeavors. In 1911, Marie was awarded the Nobel Prize in Chemistry—she was the first person to ever win two Nobel Prizes. While many were in awe, some of her male peers sought to bring her down, fueled by jealousy. Rumors spread of an affair between Marie and a married colleague. Their alleged love letters were printed in the national newspapers and Marie was depicted as a scandalous foreigner.

In the words of her daughter and first biographer, Eve, this public defamation of her character led Marie "to the brink of suicide and of madness." A member of the Nobel Prize committee wrote to her asking her not to attend the award ceremony and said she should decline the award. Marie stood up for herself and wrote back, arguing that the slander over her personal life should not affect her scientific achievements. She attended the ceremony with her eldest daughter, Irene, who would go on to win a Nobel Prize 24 years later.

A year after the scandal, Marie felt strong enough to resume her scientific work. However, her prolonged exposure to radiation resulted in many physical illnesses and led to her death in 1934. Marie's tenacity, determination, and intellect not only advanced science, but inspired generations of women to pursue science.

SPOTLIGHT ON: SCHIZOPHRENIA

WHAT IS SCHIZOPHRENIA?

Schizophrenia is a severe mental health disorder that often develops in late adolescence and impacts the way a person thinks, feels, behaves, and processes reality. Schizophrenia is related to psychosis, which means the person may experience episodes where they lose the ability to differentiate reality from delusions and hallucinations. While schizophrenia is a long-term condition and sometimes relapses occur, it is treatable and many people are able to manage their symptoms with the right treatment.

WHAT CAUSES SCHIZOPHRENIA?

The exact causes of schizophrenia remain unknown. It tends to run in families, but genetics is not the only factor. Research suggests schizophrenia is often triggered by a combination of physical, psychological, and environmental factors. If a person is already genetically at risk of schizophrenia, any stressful life event such as the loss of a loved one or abuse, can act as a trigger. Drug misuse has also been shown to increase the risk of developing schizophrenia or cause a relapse.

WHAT ARE THE SYMPTOMS OF SCHIZOPHRENIA?

There are two types of symptoms, "positive" and "negative." Positive symptoms refer to thoughts and behavioral changes such as hallucinations and delusions. During a hallucination, a person might sense (see, hear, smell, taste, or touch) something that does not exist outside of their mind. They may create a delusion to explain a hallucination. For example, if they hear a voice that only exists in their mind, they may develop a delusion, or mistaken belief, that someone is watching them. This may lead them to behave in unpredictable ways. Negative symptoms are associated with a person becoming withdrawn, exhibiting no interest in social interactions. They may appear to be emotionless. There is no specific test for schizophrenia. A diagnosis is usually made by a specialist mental health professional.

SUPPORT WHILE LIVING WITH SCHIZOPHRENIA

In many cases, a person living with schizophrenia will need a professional support network that will often include social workers, occupational therapists, and psychiatrists. The team will form a treatment plan tailored to the individual, following an assessment of the level of care required. As part of the treatment plan, the individual will learn how to spot the signs of a relapse. In the cases of severe schizophrenic episodes, the individual may need to spend some time in a psychiatric ward. Sometimes people will write advanced statements giving instructions for the treatments they would like if they experience an acute episode and are unable to make their wishes clear.

John Nash

(1928-2015)

Born in West Virginia in the USA, mathematical prodigy John Nash was the first person openly known to be living with schizophrenia to win a Nobel Prize.

John showed a remarkable talent for mathematics from a young age. He studied at Princeton University where he quickly acquired a reputation as a genius, egocentric, and eccentric. After receiving his doctorate, he moved to Boston and joined the faculty at MIT (the Massachusetts Institute of Technology) where the students called him the "Kid Professor." He began dating a nurse and had a child which he kept secret. In 1957, John married mathematician Alicia Larde. Less than two years later, while Alicia was pregnant, John experienced his first episode of psychosis. John thought he was being sent coded messages in the newspaper and began experiencing increasingly intense delusions. He described the experience in a documentary, *A Brilliant Madness*:

"[T]HE DELUSIONAL STATE OF MIND IS LIKE LIVING A DREAM. WHEN I KNEW WHERE I WAS, I WAS THERE IN OBSERVATION BUT I WAS ABLE TO THINK THAT I WAS LIKE A VICTIM OF A CONSPIRACY."

Alicia was advised to have John admitted to a psychiatric hospital where he was diagnosed with paranoid schizophrenia. Shortly after his release, he traveled to Europe and attempted to gain refugee status. John had relapsed and Alicia had to ask the authorities to track him down. He was admitted to a psychiatric hospital again. This second hospital used a regime of brutal treatments that are no longer used today. After his release, John returned to work and published a mathematical paper, but he felt unhappy. John resented Alicia for having him admitted to a hospital and, after John experienced another relapse, the couple divorced in 1962.

John's mathematical friends helped him find an apartment in Boston. He began seeing a psychiatrist weekly and took antipsychotic medication. However, a year later, he stopped taking his medication and his symptoms of paranoid schizophrenia returned. In 1970, Alicia let John move back home to support him, albeit not as husband and wife. After three decades of living with paranoid schizophrenia, John's mental health began to improve in the 1980s.

In 1994, aged 66, John was awarded a Nobel Prize for his work on game theory. He was able to return to his mathematics and teach at Princeton. Happily, John and Alicia remarried in 2001. A week before his death in 2015, John won the prestigious Abel Prize for his work on partial differential equations, becoming the first person in history to win both a Nobel Prize and the Abel Prize. John's pioneering career as a mathematician, spanning more than six decades, was full of challenges both mathematical and mental, and he showed that anything is possible when you put your mind to it.

BUZZ ALDRIN

(1930-PRESENT)

Nicknamed "Buzzer" (shortened to "Buzz") by his older sister who couldn't pronounce the word "brother," American astronaut Edwin Eugene Aldrin Junior was one of the first two humans to walk on the Moon. The Air Force psychiatrists had declared Buzz mentally and emotionally fit to be an astronaut, but no one had considered how returning from the Moon as an instant celebrity might affect a person's mental health.

Born in New Jersey, Buzz became an Air Force pilot and flew in combat missions in Korea. When he returned from the war, Buzz married Joan Archer and they had three children together. In 1963, Buzz earned a doctorate in Astronautics at MIT and was selected to be an astronaut. On 20 July 1969, Buzz landed on the Moon as part of the Apollo 11 mission, with Neil Armstrong and Michael Collins. They returned home as public heroes, but Buzz soon found life in the spotlight frustrating and unrewarding.

Buzz had always been goal-oriented, but after his return he felt directionless—what should he do next? In 1971, Buzz retired from NASA and became the commandant of the US Air Force Edwards Test Pilot School, but he didn't feel fulfilled. He fell into a depression. Buzz spent four weeks at Wilford Hall, a military hospital, where they used a combination of therapy and medication to treat his condition. After a short remission, Buzz fell back into a depression after taking early retirement in 1972. He continued to work through his feelings with doctors: Buzz had achieved so much and received countless accolades, but always being referred to as "second" to Neil had affected Buzz's mental health. Buzz also felt great sadness and disappointment not to have made the rank of Air Force general.

In 1973, Buzz published his first autobiography, *Return to Earth*, which was made into a film. He hoped his story would inspire others living with depression, and he was delighted to be asked to join the board of National Association of Mental Health (NAMH). But despite being open about his experience with depression, Buzz described in his later book, *Magnificent Desolation*, how he kept his drinking private and it became increasingly problematic: **"I MOVED FROM DRINKING TO DEPRESSION TO HEAVIER DRINKING TO A DEEPER DEPRESSION. I RECOGNIZED THE PATTERN, BUT I CONTINUALLY SABOTAGED MY OWN EFFORTS TO DO ANYTHING ABOUT IT."**

Buzz and Joan divorced in 1974 and after a short relationship and marriage to Beverley Van Zile, during which time he sought treatment for his alcoholism, Buzz married his third wife, Lois Driggs Cannon in 1988. They traveled the world together, before separating in 2011. Throughout his life, Buzz has continued to champion space travel and set up the nonprofit, ShareSpace Foundation. Buzz's openness about the successes and challenges he has faced throughout his life continues to help and inspire people around the world.

Michelle Obama

(1964-PRESENT)

Former First Lady Michelle Obama is an inspiration to people around the world. In 2009, the Obamas became the first African American family in the White House and worked tirelessly to improve healthcare across the country. Since leaving the White House, Michelle has discussed the techniques she used and continues to use to protect her mental health.

Born in Chicago, Michelle dreamed of studying at the most prestigious universities of America. Her school's college advisor said she wouldn't fit in because of the color of her skin, but Michelle proved them wrong. She studied first at Princeton and then Harvard University, graduating as a lawyer. She went to work at Sidley Austin law firm where she met Barack Obama. They married in 1992 and had two daughters. When Barack decided to run for resident, Michelle stood alongside him, supporting his campaign. As first lady, Michelle opened up conversations about health and wellbeing. This led to the "Let's Move" initiative to keep children healthy. Since leaving the White House, Michelle has continued to speak out about wellbeing, including her own.

In 2020, Michelle experienced low-grade depression. In a candid podcast, she explained that there had been a number of factors that had impacted her mental health: the isolation of lockdown during the COVID-19 pandemic, the dispirited feeling she felt when witnessing the actions of the Trump administration, and the racial strife in America. Speaking out on social media, after the deaths of George Floyd, an African American man who was murdered by a white police officer in Minnesota on May 25, 2020, Michelle wrote:

"I'M EXHAUSTED BY A HEARTBREAK THAT NEVER SEEMS TO STOP. RIGHT NOW IT'S GEORGE [FLOYD], BREONNA [TAYLOR], AND AHMAUD [ARBERY]. BEFORE THAT IT WAS ERIC [GARNER], SANDRA [BLAND], AND MICHAEL [BROWN]. IT JUST GOES ON, AND ON, AND ON. RACISM IS A REALITY THAT SO MANY OF US GROW UP LEARNING TO JUST DEAL WITH."

Michelle knew she needed to take steps to look after her mental health. The key tool for her was having a routine. She also made sure to exercise and spend time outside. Michelle spoke of how sometimes she turns off her phone for a while, stepping away from the negative energy of the news.

Michelle's podcast is a reminder that each and every one of us has mental health, in the same way we have physical health. Not everyone lives with a clinically diagnosed mental health disorder, but we all have mental health. Michelle encourages everyone to find the self-care tools that bring them joy, calm, and peace and enable them to navigate the challenges life presents.

Michelle continues to be one of the most influential and inspirational people in the world. Her multimillion bestselling memoir, *Becoming,* was turned into a documentary in 2020.

David Chang

(1977-PRESENT)

Asian American celebrity chef David Chang is the mastermind behind the Momofuku culinary empire. In his memoir, *Eat a Peach*, David explains how the idea was born from his depression which "manifests itself as an addiction to work."

Born in Virginia in the USA to deeply religious Korean parents, David was a golf prodigy and wanted nothing more than to make his parents proud. Eventually the pressure to live up to his father's expectations took its toll and David came to hate the sport. Trying to fit in with his white American classmates, David developed a sense of shame and anxiety about Korean food. In his memoir, he describes experiencing a sense of "otherness" and the Korean emotion "han" (there is no English translation for this emotion—it is a complex mix of grief, rage, and resentment deriving from cultural injustice).

After finishing school, David traveled to Japan to teach English, hoping to find a sense of belonging. But he didn't find it and experienced his first manic episode. He returned to America and, after an unhappy corporate job, enrolled in culinary school. Afterwards, he worked in two high-pressure kitchens where he began to doubt his ability. When his mother's breast cancer reoccurred he experienced his first depressive episode. He sought the professional help of Dr Eliot, who diagnosed him with bipolar disorder.

David's depression made him feel like he had nothing to lose, and so in 2004, he decided to open a noodle bar in New York, Momofuku (which means "Lucky Peach" in Japanese). To his surprise, his father, who had always been against his culinary career, offered to support him. The early days in the restaurant were tough and full of practical and mental challenges. Through a combination of risk-taking, perseverance, a talented team, and good fortune, the restaurant was soon thriving and David went on to open more critically acclaimed restaurants, each with their own unique style. David believes his restaurants saved his life, but he also knows that **"COOKING BRINGS OUT THE BEST AND WORST"** in him. While he found a sense of purpose in the repetitive tasks, failures in the kitchen hit him hard and his staff often took the force of his emotional swings. During his career, he has experienced panic attacks, anxiety, and rage in the kitchen, as well as opened new restaurants during periods of mania.

In 2018, David and his wife Grace found out she was pregnant. The day before, David's friend and fellow chef Anthony Bourdain had died by suicide. It spurred David to take the brave step of sharing his mental health experiences publicly to help other chefs in the industry. In 2019, having opened restaurants all over the world, David stepped down as Momofuku CEO and a year later released his memoir in which he shares that one of his hopes for the future is the end of stigma around mental health.

SPOTLIGHT ON: BIPOLAR DISORDER

WHAT IS BIPOLAR DISORDER?

Formerly known as manic depression, bipolar disorder is a mental health disorder that causes a person to experience unusual and extreme shifts in moods, energy, sleep patterns, and ability to concentrate. Unlike typical highs and lows that people experience, bipolar disorder causes extreme mood states that can significantly impact a person's life, from overly high and energetic states ("mania") to extreme states of sadness or hopelessness ("depression"). The length, intensity, and frequency of the mood swings varies from person to person, but may last weeks, months, or even years. Some people can experience rapid mood cycling with daily or even intraday mood swings, or mixed mood episodes, meaning they can experience both manic and depressive symptoms at the same time.

WHAT CAUSES BIPOLAR DISORDER?

The exact causes are unknown, but there is evidence that people with a family history of bipolar disorder are more likely to develop the condition. Research also suggests that episodes of mania and depression can be triggered by stress, big life events, and feeling overwhelmed by problems.

MANIA

During episodes of mania, a person may feel extremely happy and energetic, often coming up with ambitious ideas and sometimes spending more money than they can afford. They may speak very fast or go for long periods of time without sleeping and eating. They may be easily distracted, irritable, or agitated. Some people may develop an overinflated sense of self-importance and in some cases may experience psychosis such as delusions and hallucinations. Friends and family may become aware that the person is acting out of character, taking more risks. This manic phase of bipolar disorder can sometimes lead to disastrous physical and financial consequences. Some people with bipolar disorder experience hypomania, which is a milder form of mania.

DEPRESSION

During episodes of depression, a person may experience feelings of emptiness, sadness, hopelessness, and low self-esteem. Often, people experience a loss of interest in things they would usually enjoy and may feel tearful, guilt-ridden, irritable, or moody. These feelings might make a person avoid seeing family and friends. Physical symptoms may include tiredness, aches and pains, and routine tasks such as getting dressed and making decisions may feel much harder. Some may experience a loss of appetite, while others may overeat. Severe depression can cause thoughts of self-harm or suicide.

ANDREW FLINTOFF

(1977-PRESENT)

Better known as Freddie (or Fred), Andrew Flintoff is a former England captain and cricketing legend. Since retiring from cricket with a knee injury in 2010, Freddie has gone on to become a successful broadcaster and TV presenter. He has used his platform to expose the stigma of mental health disorders in sport.

Born in Lancashire, Freddie began playing county cricket as a young boy. In 1998 he made his cricket test debut for England and by 2003 Freddie had become an established member of the England team. What nobody knew was that Freddie was secretly living with an eating disorder, bulimia. His eating disorder was triggered when the press claimed his weight gain had caused a dip in his form. Freddie suddenly became acutely aware of his weight and that everyone else was aware of it too. He began to purge (deliberately make himself sick) after meals and lost three stone. But just as his mental health was deteriorating, Freddie's cricket improved. This started a vicious cycle: suddenly his former critics were praising him for his new trimmed appearance and return to form.

In 2005, Freddie was instrumental in England's victory over Australia at the Ashes. He was made England captain in 2006, but after a disappointing Ashes series he was demoted to vice-captain and his bulimia worsened. The only person Freddie confided in was his wife, Rachael. Despite her being supportive, Freddie didn't tell her the full extent of his bulimia. When a dietician came to speak to the cricket team, Freddie planned to ask for help. Before he got a chance, the dietician reinforced the stigma that only women experience eating disorders. Freddie said nothing. It would be more than a decade before Freddie took the brave step to speak out about his eating disorder in his BBC documentary *Living with Bulimia*.

During this documentary, Freddie spoke to other men living with bulimia. He reflected on his own experience and how he uses exercise to curb his urge to purge: **"IF I DON'T GET TO TRAIN, I DON'T FEEL GREAT, AND I CAN GET VERY DOWN. BUT UNTIL NOW I DIDN'T KNOW THAT COULD BE PART OF MY BULIMIA."**

Through his conversations with health professionals, Freddie discovered that overexercising is also a symptom of bulimia. For Freddie, not 20 minutes goes by without him thinking about his weight—it is exhausting.

Freddie has used his position in the public eye to highlight how stigma around men living with eating disorders can make it feel like asking for help is a weakness, when in fact it is a strength. As a result of his documentary, Freddie intends to seek professional treatment for his condition. Freddie has received an MBE for his contribution to English cricket and continues to shine in his entertainment career.

Serena Williams
(1981-PRESENT)

The youngest of five sisters, Serena Williams grew up in Los Angeles playing tennis with her sister, Venus. Coached by their father, tennis was very much a family affair. Later in life, Serena would reflect on the various pressures she felt to play tennis and how this impacted her mental health.

Serena was always in her big sister's "tennis shadow" as a child. Venus was stronger, taller, and fiercer on the court. But it just made Serena even more determined to work hard and up her game. The hard work paid off and, in 2002, Serena became the world-number-one female tennis player and looked unstoppable. However, in 2003 a knee injury meant that Serena had to pull out of several tournaments and shortly afterwards her eldest sister, Yetunde, was killed by gun violence. This, combined with the pressure to impress her new commercial sponsor and regain her number-one ranking, led Serena to slip into a depression. In her autobiography, *My Life: Queen of the Court*, Serena described feeling "an aching sadness" and "a sudden disinterest" in the world around her, particularly in tennis.

Usually, Serena would speak to her family all the time, but she shut them out. Soon, the only time she left her house was to see her therapist. Through the sessions, she realized she was exhausted from trying to please everyone else. By 2006, Serena felt a growing resentment towards tennis and her world ranking dropped to 140. When Serena finally opened up to her family about how she'd been feeling, she was able to start the path to recovery. Serena realized she needed to learn how to make herself happy before she could make other people happy. Then she went on a life-changing goodwill trip to Africa with her family and connected with her heritage. Serena spent some time re-evaluating her life goals and chose to play tennis because she wanted to. It was the turning point that started her tennis comeback.

Serena regained her number one world ranking in 2013 and held it for 186 consecutive weeks until a couple of shock defeats in 2016. Again, Serena demonstrated strong mental strength and competitive spirit, defeating her sister Venus in the 2017 Australian Open final to claim her 23rd Grand Slam singles title—a new record in the Open Era of tennis. A few months later, Serena revealed that she had been pregnant when she won! Serena and her husband, Alexis, welcomed their daughter into the world on 1 September 2017. In her docuseries, *Being Serena*, she bravely opened up about her postnatal emotional experience, finding the balance between motherhood and her return to tennis. Alongside being one of the world's greatest ever female tennis players, Serena has worked as an actress and founded a fashion company and the Yetunde Price Resource Center charity.

Jameela Jamil

(1986-PRESENT)

Born in England, Jameela is a one-of-a-kind multi-hyphenate who works as an actress, writer, host, and advocate. Fueled by her personal experiences, Jameela created the activism platform, I Weigh.

Growing up isn't easy in general, but being a young British South Asian girl in London who had medical issues as a child, Jameela experienced teasing and bullying as well as fatphobia. Aged 11, Jameela and her classmates had to weigh themselves as part of a maths lesson on data collection. Everyone laughed when Jameela was revealed as the heaviest in the class. Mortified, Jameela told her parents who "panicked and expressed shame" and immediately put Jameela on a "crash diet." Feeling alone and surrounded by fatphobia at school and celebrities on TV, Jameela developed an eating disorder.

"I WOULD PASS OUT FROM LACK OF NUTRITION... I WAS DEPRESSED. I WAS WEAK. I WAS IN CHAOS."

While living with body dysmorphia as a teenager, Jameela worked as a model, which made the problems even worse. However, after a car accident left her temporarily in a wheelchair at the age of 17, she gained weight and stopped modeling. Instead, she began teaching English at an international school. However, Jameela returned to the public eye at the age of 22 presenting a children's TV show. She went on to have an impressive eight-year TV and radio career in the UK. Despite being told she was "too old, too ethnic, and too fat" to make it in Los Angeles, Jameela decided to move to the US. She proved her critics wrong by securing a US TV sitcom role from her very first audition in Hollywood, in *The Good Place* which became a huge success.

But for all the wonderful opportunities the entertainment industry has offered, Jameela is no stranger to the toxic side of the industry. During her career, Jameela has also had her ethnicity airbrushed out of photoshoots, lightening her skin tone to make her look more Caucasian, and Jameela has spoken out about the impact this has not only on her but on the false ideals of beauty it teaches the youth of today.

Jameela is an advocate for many causes and in 2018 launched a movement and activism platform called I Weigh. What started as an idea and an Instagram page became a platform and community of changemakers who come together to share ideas, experiences, and ultimately mobilize activism. Through original content, editorial, and podcasts, the platform explores social issues that stem from mental health to climate change to the representation of marginalized groups.

SPOTLIGHT ON: EATING DISORDERS

WHAT ARE EATING DISORDERS?

Eating disorders are a range of conditions that are characterized by a serious disturbance in thoughts, feelings, and behaviors around eating, food, body shape, or weight. Anyone can develop an eating disorder, at any age, but they are particularly prevalent in adolescents.

ANOREXIA NERVOSA

People living with anorexia often view themselves as overweight, even when they are severely underweight. Due to their intense preoccupation with food and body weight or shape, they may restrict their food intake, exercise obsessively, or weigh themselves repeatedly. They may take appetite suppressants or laxatives to try to avoid gaining weight. They may develop strict rituals around eating and skip meals.

BINGE EATING DISORDER

People living with BED regularly eat a lot of food in a short space of time, known as "binging." Often they will experience intense feelings of guilt and shame after a binge session. They will typically eat alone, very fast, and even when they're not hungry. They may try to hide how much they eat from others. In some cases, a person will gain a lot of weight, leading to obesity and type 2 diabetes.

BULIMIA

People living with bulimia have recurrent episodes of uncontrollably eating large amounts of food, followed by behaviors that compensate, such as forced vomiting, use of laxatives, and/ or excessive exercise. They often engage in this behavior secretively, making it harder for friends and family to notice the signs. The binging-purging cycle can be triggered by hunger, sadness, or stress. Like all eating disorders, there are many serious side effects, such as dental problems and poor health.

ARFID

Avoidant/restrictive food intake disorder is a condition where a person avoids eating specific food. This is not the same as a person going on a special diet to lose weight. It may occur if a person has had a bad experience with that food such as choking, or negative feelings towards the food such as its smell, taste, or texture.

OSFED

Other specified feeding or eating disorder is a blanket term used for individuals who display symptoms of an eating disorder, but do not fully align with anorexia, BED, or bulimia. The majority of people with an eating disorder are experiencing OSFED.

CAUSES OF EATING DISORDERS

The exact causes are unknown. Research suggests that a person is more likely to develop an eating disorder if there is a family history. Other factors include anxiety, low self-esteem, sexual abuse, or a perfectionist mindset. A person may be more likely to develop an eating disorder if they have been criticized for their weight or eating habit. Peer pressure or social expectations can also be a trigger. For example, a person may feel they need to be slim to play a particular sport or wear a certain type of clothing.

SYMPTOMS OF EATING DISORDERS

Psychological symptoms include a fear of putting on weight, constantly thinking about food, changes in mood, and a critical view of their body. Feelings of guilt and shame are common, as well as feeling a lack of control over eating and anxiety. Physical symptoms include exhaustion, constipation, and in some cases self-harm. The long-term physical health implications are very serious. Eating disorders can cause starvation and a person may experience physical symptoms such as a dangerously low body mass index (BMI), exhaustion, dizziness, hair loss, dry skin, muscle weakness, osteoporosis, infertility, heart complications, seizures, memory loss, kidney and bowel problems, and a weakened immune system.

DEEPIKA PADUKONE

(1986-PRESENT)

Indian actress, producer, and fashion icon, Deepika Padukone was ranked in *TIME* magazine's 100 most influential people in the world in 2018. Alongside her phenomenal on-screen success, Deepika has become a mental health ambassador, setting up her own foundation and sharing her personal experiences with depression.

Deepika grew up with her family in Mumbai. Her father was a professional badminton player and Deepika played to a high standard as a child, but gave it up at the age of 16 to focus on acting. She moved to Bangalore in 2005 and debuted in her first Bollywood film, *Om Shanti Om*, in 2007. In 2013, Deepika starred in four of the six highest-grossing Bollywood movies of the year and became one of the top-ten highest-paid actresses in the world. But while Deepika should have been feeling elated about the success of her rising career, she was about to enter a period of intense depression.

Deepika can clearly recall the morning of 15 February 2014, when she woke up with a strange feeling she'd never experienced before. She felt empty and directionless and soon began experiencing bouts of unexplainable crying. In the days that followed, she remembers having to smile in public, while secretly crying in a bathroom.

Her emotions swung like a pendulum, alternating from feeling okay to feeling low.

"FOR SOMEONE WHO LOVES TO MULTITASK, MAKING DECISIONS SUDDENLY FELT LIKE A BURDEN. WAKING UP EVERY MORNING HAD BECOME A STRUGGLE. I WAS EXHAUSTED AND OFTEN THOUGHT OF GIVING UP."

Deepika didn't know what was happening. She wondered whether it was a phase that would pass. But her mother, Ujjala, recognized the symptoms of depression that Deepika was experiencing because she had seen other family members go through it. It was her mother who encouraged her to get professional help.

Deepika began working with a psychiatrist, who officially diagnosed her with anxiety and depression. He explained to her that seeking help is a sign of strength. Deepika was so incredibly strong that she decided to share her story on national TV to help break down mental health stigma in India. Deepika considers herself very fortunate to have had her family's support.

As a result of her experience, Deepika wanted to find a way to support others living with depression. In 2015, Deepika founded LiveLoveLaugh, which supports people living with stress, anxiety, and depression. Three years later, she married Indian actor Ranveer Singh. Deepika continues to reach new heights in her acting career as well as being a mental health advocate.

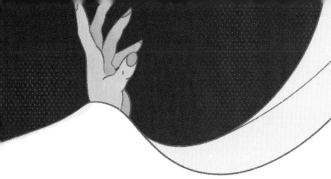

LESLEY CHIANG

(1986-PRESENT)

Singer-songwriter, actress and mental health advocate Lesley Chiang grew up in Canada. She comes from a family of actors and producers, including her grandparents (Hua Yan and Wei Hong), uncles (Derek Yee and David Chiang), and father, Paul Chun. Lesley was known for her positive, happy-go-lucky personality. But in 2014, she developed a mental health disorder that nearly ended her life.

Lesley knew she wanted to sing and act from the age of three. She entered the entertainment business in Japan at 19 and made her film debut in *Shinjuku Incident*. In 2010, Lesley debuted as a singer with her brother as "Benji and Lesley." A year later, she launched her solo music career, alongside acting. But just as her career was taking off, Lesley entered a very emotional period of life.

In 2014, Lesley broke up with her boyfriend and she felt sad. At first, this felt like the type of sadness to be expected after a relationship ends. But gradually her sadness deepened into a sense of worthlessness and her life felt meaningless: **"IT SEEMED LIKE EVERYTHING I DID PROVED EVEN MORE TO MYSELF THAT I WAS GARBAGE AND JUST LIKE GARBAGE I NEEDED TO BE DISPOSED OF."**

One night, Lesley felt like she no longer wanted to be alive. But she wanted to write one last song first about how she was feeling. As the lyrics began to take shape, she started thinking about the musical accompaniments the song could have. Slowly her focus moved away from suicidal thoughts to the music. The song was called "Tonight" and it saved her life. However, she would still go on to experience suicidal thoughts in two other periods over the next four years—which she overcame with her brother's support. In 2015, Lesley was diagnosed with severe clinical depression. She also experiences anxiety and panic attacks. With the help and support of her family, Lesley has learned to manage her mental health disorders.

In 2019, she shared the strategies she uses to manage her mental health disorders. Firstly, she gave her depression a name, "Borat." Being able to visualize her depression and also give it a personality helped her to fight back. "Borat" is a "pathological liar" so when her Borat (aka her depression) calls her worthless, she knows not to believe it. Alongside exercising, practicing self-care, and getting quality sleep, Lesley uses a number system to support her wellbeing. Every day, Lesley writes down a number from 1 to 10 to score the level of anxiety and depression she is experiencing. Her trusted loved ones look at these scores each day, which helps them know how to support her. One of her biggest supporters is her partner, Pakho. Lesley continues to grow her entertainment career, acting in *Anniversary*, *Lucky Fat Man*, and *Lo and Behold* as well as releasing new music, including "Tonight."

Alok Vaid-Menon

(1991-PRESENT)

Alok Vaid-Menon is an Indian-American gender nonconforming, transfeminine writer, and performance artist. Growing up in a small conservative town in Texas, Alok was severely harassed for being a "boy" who was "too feminine," which led them to experience extreme depression. Alok used art as a way to heal. Through their art and public speaking, Alok has become an LGBTQIA+ role model as well as a mental health advocate.

The Indian community where Alok grew up was so small, it was like a family. Every weekend, Alok sang and danced at joyful family dinner parties, dressed up in their mother's and sister's clothes, as their extended family cheered them on. So, when Alok was around six, they didn't think twice about dancing in the school talent show. But everyone laughed—the children mistook Alok for a boy and they believed boys didn't dance. It was the first time Alok felt shame.

Alok was severely bullied throughout their childhood. Alok couldn't speak up about the harassment they were experiencing without "outing" themselves. Friends and family suggested they tried to "act less feminine," but this only made Alok feel worse. Rather than embracing Alok's femininity, they too were trying to repress Alok's freedom to express themself. Alok began wearing less colorful clothes in an attempt to fit in. But the more Alok tried to conform to their classmates' binary understanding of gender, the more shame they felt. In their book, *Beyond the Gender Binary*, Alok described the potential danger of feeling shame: **"THE THING ABOUT SHAME IS THAT IT EATS AT YOU UNTIL IT FULLY CONSUMES YOU... IT'S NOT JUST THAT YOU INTERNALIZE THE SHAME; RATHER, IT BECOMES YOU."**

Alok felt alone and scared. They began experiencing severe depression and suicidal thoughts, which led to an attempt to take their own life as a teenager. At the time, Alok didn't have any role models—they didn't know what trans and nonbinary meant.

At 18, Alok came out to their family. They left Texas and studied Feminist, Gender, and Sexuality Studies at Stanford University where they surrounded themself with similar-minded people. At last, Alok had the freedom to rediscover themself and wear the clothes they loved. But just as Alok finally felt comfortable in their own skin, a new problem emerged. Alok experienced more violent abuse for walking down the street in a dress. But Alok stood proud. They had come to realize that: **"SHAME IS JOY INTERRUPTED."**

Each and every one of us deserves to live in our own unique joy. Alok found the strength to use their voice to fight for equality. As a mixed-media artist, Alok explores themes of trauma and belonging. In 2019, Alok returned to their hometown to host a PRIDE party, marking the 50th anniversary of the Stonewall riots, an important event in the fight for LGBTQIA+ rights.

GRETA THUNBERG

(2003-PRESENT)

Swedish climate activist Greta Thunberg first heard about global warming when she was around eight years old. It didn't make sense to her: if global warming was really as bad as it sounded, why wasn't everybody working to stop it? Aged 11, Greta fell into a depression. She stopped eating and soon after stopped speaking.

It wasn't just the planet's climate that was in crisis—the Thunberg family was, too. Greta's parents tried everything they could to make their daughter eat. They kept a food diary. Sometimes it would take over two hours for Greta to eat just five pieces of gnocchi. Together, the children's psychiatry service and the Stockholm Centre for Eating Disorders diagnosed Greta with Asperger syndrome on the autism spectrum and selective mutism (she only speaks when she feels it is necessary to speak). Alongside her eating disorder and depression, the doctors also diagnosed Greta with obsessive-compulsive disorder (OCD).

After two months of barely eating, Greta lost around ten kilograms of weight. The doctors told her she might have to be hospitalized or her lack of nutrition could be fatal. Then, Greta spoke. She told her parents she was going to try to start eating again. But it was a slow process. Greta focussed her energy on climate change, keeping a copy of every article she found in the media. There weren't many. No one was talking about climate change and Greta knew that something needed to be done. Aged 15, Greta decided to go on strike outside of parliament in the three weeks running up to the 2018 Swedish general election.

It wasn't easy as the family described in their autobiography, *Our House is on Fire*. Greta showed great mental strength and tenacity to plan and carry out her strike. She talked to fellow activists and journalists and she ate in front of strangers, something she had rarely done over the past few years. She was "making her way towards the time before OCD and eating disorders. Or rather. To the time after." As news spread of Greta's campaign, more and more people came to strike with her. One day, a whole class of students stopped to speak to her. Greta panicked and cried. Later, she explained to them: **"I'VE NEVER MET A GROUP OF CHILDREN THAT HASN'T BEEN MEAN TO ME. AND WHEREVER I'VE BEEN I'VE BEEN BULLIED BECAUSE I'M DIFFERENT."**

Even after the three-week strike, Greta still felt she could do more and so she decided to strike every Friday. It became known as "Fridays for Future" and millions of children have taken part all over the world. Since then, Greta has spoken in front of global audiences and world leaders, continuing to fight to save our planet.

SPOTLIGHT ON: ANXIETY

WHAT IS AN ANXIETY DISORDER?

It is natural to feel anxious at times—everyone does. But if a person begins to experience high levels of anxiety that affects their daily life, it may be a sign of an anxiety disorder. It is important to be able to differentiate between fear, worry, anxiety, and panic. Fear is the body's instinctive reaction to perceived dangers and often triggers a fight-or-flight-or-freeze response. Worry is the anticipation of a fearful event. Anxiety is an overwhelming sense of worry or fear. Panic is a severe form of anxiety.

GENERALIZED ANXIETY DISORDER (GAD)

This is often a long-term condition in which a person can experience persistent or excessive worry or fear over anything, at any time. Depending on the severity of the anxiety, the condition can have a significant impact on a person's ability to do basic daily tasks. They may feel restless and have trouble concentrating or sleeping. Like with all anxiety disorders, a person may experience heart palpitations and dizziness.

WHAT CAUSES ANXIETY DISORDERS?

The exact causes are unknown and often there is no clear reason why someone developed clinical anxiety when they did. Research suggests that clinical anxiety could be the reaction to a traumatic event that happened in their past. A person with a family history of generalized anxiety is five times more likely to develop GAD themselves.

SPECIFIC PHOBIAS

A phobia is a fear over a specific thing. This could be
an animal, location, event, object, or feeling. Each phobia has
an individual name: for example arachnophobia is the fear of spiders;
claustrophobia is the fear of enclosed spaces; acrophobia is the fear of
heights; trypanophobia is the fear of needles; and there are many, many
more. Just thinking about the thing they fear can cause a person living with
a phobia to experience anxiety or a panic attack. Phobias can have a severe
impact on an individual's daily life. They may feel isolated or avoid certain
situations that they worry will cause anxiety.

SOCIAL ANXIETY DISORDER
(SOCIAL PHOBIA)

This condition causes an individual to feel overwhelmingly worried and
anxious about social interactions. They may worry others are judging them
and have low self-esteem and avoid social situations.

PANIC DISORDER

A person living with panic disorder will regularly experience anxiety and
panic attacks, often for no clear reason. Typically lasting five to twenty
minutes, panic attacks are caused by a rush of adrenaline, and can result
in a range of symptoms such as racing heartbeat, shortness of breath,
chest pain, shaking, sweating, and nausea, as well as a sense of dread or
imminent death. During a panic attack, people are advised to take
slow, deep breaths, focus on something positive, and remember
the attack is not life-threatening and will pass.

SPOTLIGHT ON: TREATMENTS

Everyone's mental health is individual. There is no one-size-fits-all approach to treating and managing mental health disorders. Recovery can take time, but is possible with the right treatment. People who live with a mental health condition should consider speaking to a health professional who can create a tailored a treatment plan for their specific needs. Often a combination of different treatments is required.

COGNITIVE BEHAVIORAL THERAPY (CBT)

"Cognition" is about how we think, "behavior" is about how we act. Cognitive behavioral therapy (CBT) is a talking therapy that equips a person with a set of tools and techniques to adapt the way they think about—and consequently react to—problems. CBT breaks down our emotional experience into three parts: thoughts, feelings, and behaviors. Sometimes, the brain can develop unhelpful, negative thought patterns that can impact a person's emotional state, such as: all-or-nothing thinking, over-generalizing, catastrophizing, and jumping to conclusions. Negative thought patterns can distort the reality of situations and make a person feel overly anxious, scared, or sad, which can in turn lead to panic attacks, depression, and other unwanted behavioral and emotional responses. By challenging negative thoughts and developing positive patterns of thought, a person can learn to manage their feelings and behaviors. CBT often involves "homework" because it is not a quick fix. It can be a particularly effective treatment for anxiety and depression.

OTHER TYPES OF THERAPY

DIALECTICAL BEHAVIOR THERAPY (DBT) is a modified form of CBT which can help people experiencing suicidal thoughts. It may also be used to treat people living with eating disorders, bipolar disorder, and PTSD. In **GROUP THERAPY**, several people living with mental health disorders meet with a therapist and support each other. **FAMILY THERAPY** focusses on helping family members learn how to best support and communicate with their loved one who lives with a mental health disorder. **ART THERAPY** is about learning to express yourself and your emotions through painting and other forms of art. Children may be offered **PLAY THERAPY**, which helps children to find ways to talk about their emotions and feelings through playing games with toys.

MEDICATION

There are various forms of medication that may
be prescribed by healthcare professionals such as anti-anxiety
medication, antidepressants, and antipsychotics. People living with bipolar
disorder may be prescribed mood stabilizers throughout their life. Medication
can result in side effects, which should be discussed and monitored by a medical
professional to make sure the right tailored treatment plan is in place. Often, medication
will be prescribed alongside other forms of treatment such as talking therapies.

EYE MOVEMENT DESENSITIZATION AND REPROCESSING

Eye movement desensitization and reprocessing (EMDR) is often used as a treatment for
PTSD. The aim of EMDR is to help the brain reprocess the traumatic memory, so that
the person can eventually recall the memory without any negative physical or emotional
reactions. During EMDR, a person recalls the details of the trauma and the negative belief or
feelings they have about the memory. They then create a positive affirmation to counteract
the negative feelings. At this point, the medical health professional will guide them through
the process of moving their eyes in a certain way, known as "bilateral (side-to-side) eye
movement." This bilateral stimulation is believed to help the brain re-assign the positive
affirmation to the traumatic memory.

PSYCHOEDUCATION

Psychoeducation equips the person with knowledge about their mental health condition, as
well as educating their family and friends. By learning to recognize the warning signs of their
mental health disorder, people can seek help before their symptoms become too severe.

EMOTIONAL WELLBEING AND MINDFULNESS

Not everyone lives with a clinically diagnosed mental health disorder, but we all have mental
health. Our mental health can be strengthened by developing regular routines, exercise,
healthy eating, and mindfulness, which involves taking quality time to relax and focus on the
present moment. Some people practice yoga or meditate to grow their sense of awareness of
the world around them. Others keep a gratitude diary, noting down three happy things that
occurred that day. The key to mindfulness is to do it so often it becomes second nature.

USEFUL LINKS

www.ymhproject.org

www.nhs.uk/every-mind-matters   www.mind.org.uk

www.youngminds.org.uk   www.childline.org.uk

www.anxietyuk.org.uk   www.bipolaruk.org

www.beateatingdisorders.co.uk

GLOSSARY

ACCOLADE Acknowledgement of someone's work.

ADVOCATE A person who publicly supports or recommends a particular cause or policy.

ASPERGER SYNDROME A neurodevelopmental disorder characterized by difficulties in social interaction and nonverbal communication, restricted and repetitive patterns of behavior and interests.

BINARY Relating to, composed of, or involving two things.

BODY DYSMORPHIA A mental health condition where you spend a lot of time worrying about perceived flaws in your appearance.

CHRONIC Something that continues for a long time, or comes back regularly.

DETRIMENTAL Causing harm.

DEFAMATION The action of damaging someone's good reputation.

DIAGNOSE To identify the nature of an illness/ medical condition by examining the symptoms.

DISPOSITION A person's inherent qualities of mind and character.

FATPHOBIA Fear or dislike of obese people or obesity.

GENDER NONCONFORMING A person whose behavior or gender expression does not match societal expectations of their gender.

HYPERAROUSAL The flight-or-fight response kicks into high alert as a result of a traumatic event.

INSOMNIA Difficulty falling or staying asleep.

LEUCOTOMY A surgical operation involving cutting into the prefrontal lobe of the brain, formerly used to treat mental health disorders.

LGBTQIA+ An inclusive term covering people of all genders and sexualities including those who identify as lesbian, gay, bisexual, transgender, queer, intersex, asexual, and more.

MANIA A mental health condition typically marked by periods of great excitement, overactivity and sometimes delusions.

MANIC Showing wild excitement and/ or energy.

MARGINALIZED When a person, group, or concept is treated as insignificant.

METICULOUS Showing great attention to detail.

NEURODEVELOPMENTAL Relating to or involving the development of the nervous system.

NEURODIVERSITY The range of differences in individual brain function and behavioral traits.

NEUROTYPICAL A term used to describe individuals with brain functions, behaviors, and processing considered standard or typical.

NONBINARY An umbrella term for gender identities that are neither male nor female.

OSTEOPOROSIS A medical condition in which the bones become brittle and fragile from loss of tissue.

OTHERNESS The quality/ fact of being different.

PALPITATIONS A noticeably fast, strong, and irregular heartbeat due to agitation, exertion, or illness.

PARANOID Thinking and feeling like you are being threatened even if there is little/ no evidence that you are.

PENSIVE Engaged in or reflecting in deep or serious thought.

PHOBIA Extreme or irrational fear of an aversion to something.

POSTNATAL The period after the birth of a child.

PSYCHIATRY The study and treatment of mental health, emotional disturbance, and abnormal behavior.

PSYCHOSIS Where you see or hear things that are not there (hallucinations) or believe things that are not true (delusions).

PURGE To get rid of an unwanted food, quality, condition, or feeling.

RELAPSE When health worsens after a temporary period of improvement.

REMISSION The reduction or disappearance of the signs and/ or symptoms of a disease.

RETROSPECTIVE Looking back on or dealing with past events or situations.

SCIATICA Pain caused by an irritated nerve, affecting your back, hip, and the outer side of the leg.

SELF-CARE To take an active role in protecting one's wellbeing and happiness through action.

SLANDER To make false and damaging statements about someone.

STIGMA A set of negative and unfair beliefs based on a prominent characteristic such as mental health disorders, race or disability.

TEMPERAMENT An aspect of someone's personality concerned with their nature, which affects their moods.

TRANSFEMININE A person whose gender identity is partially or fully feminine and differs from the sex identified/ assigned at birth.

TRAUMA A deeply distressing and disturbing experience.

TRIGGER Something that affects a person's emotional state.

WEAKNESS The state of being weak, having little physical strength and/ or being fragile. Mental health conditions are not a sign of weakness.

WITHDRAWN Not wanting to communicate with others.

INDEX

abuse 5, 6, 20, 30, 49, 55
actresses 44-45, 46-47, 50-53
adrenaline 20, 58
agoraphobia 15
alcohol 21, 35
Aldrin, Buzz 34-35
Andersen, Hans Christian 10-11
anorexia nervosa 13, 48-49
antidepressants 61
antipsychotics 33, 61
anxiety 7, 15, 19-21, 39, 49, 51, 53, 58-61
anxiety disorders 58-59
appetite loss 5, 12, 19, 41
artists 4-5, 24-25, 54-55
Asperger syndrome 57
astronaut 34-35
authors/writers 10-11, 14-15, 22-23
autism 5, 7, 27, 57
avoidant/restrictive food intake disorder (ARFID) 49
binge eating disorder (BED) 48
bipolar disorder 13, 17, 19, 25, 39-41, 60-61
body dysmorphia 47
bulimia 43, 48-49
bullying 6, 12, 47, 55, 57

Chang, David 38-39
chef 38-39
Chiang, Lesley 52-53
climate activist 56-57
cognitive behavioural therapy (CBT) 60
COVID-19 37
cricket 42-43
Curie, Marie 28-29

Darwin, Charles 14-15
delusions 9, 30-31, 33, 40
depression 5, 7, 9, 11-12, 17, 19-20, 23, 35, 37, 39-41, 45, 47, 50-51, 53, 55, 57, 60
dialectical behaviour therapy (DBT) 60
drug misuse 21, 30

eating disorders 13, 43, 47-49, 57, 60
exercise 37, 43, 48, 61
eye movement desensitisation and reprcessing (EMDR) 60-61

family therapy 60
fatphobia 47
flashbacks 19, 21
Flintoff, Andrew 42-43

generalised anxiety disorder (GAD) 58, 59

gratitude diary 61
group therapy 60

hallucinations 30-31, 40
hypomania 40

I Weigh 47
inventors 22-23, 26-27
irritable 12, 19, 21, 40-41
Jamil, Jameela 46-47

language to describe mental health 13
life events 6, 12, 30, 41
LiveLoveLaugh 51
loneliness 9, 11-12, 23, 25
Lovelace, Ada 16-17

mania 17, 39-41
mathematicians 8-9, 16-17, 28-29, 32-33, 47
medication 33, 35, 60-61
meditation 61
mental health, looking after 37, 53, 61
Michelangelo 4-5
mindfulness 61
model 46-47
mood stabilisers 61

Nash, John 32-33
Newton, Sir Isaac 8-9
Nightingale, Florence 18-19
Nobel, Alfred 22-23
Nobel Prizes 23, 29, 33

nurses 18-19, 33

Obama, Michelle 36-37
obsessive compulsive disorder (OCD) 5, 6-7, 13, 27, 57, 61
occupational therapist 31
other specified feeding or eating disorder (OSFED) 49
overeating 12, 41, 48
overwhelmed 41, 58-59

Padukone, Deepika 50-51
panic attacks 39, 53, 58, 59, 60
panic disorder 15, 58
perfectionism 5, 49
phobias 15, 27, 47, 59
physical health problems 23, 29, 49
post-traumatic stress disorder (PTSD) 19-21, 60-61
psychiatrist 31, 33, 35, 51
psychiatry 23, 57
psychoeducation 60-61
psychosis 9, 25, 30, 33, 40

racism 37

schizophrenia 13, 30-31, 33
scientists 8-9, 14-15, 22-23, 26-29

self-care 21, 37, 53, 60
self-esteem 12, 27, 41, 49, 59
self-harm 12, 21, 41
ShareSpace Foundation 35
sleeping difficulties 7, 9, 21, 40, 58
social anxiety disorder (social phobia) 59
social worker 31
sportspeople 42-45
stigma 13, 39, 43, 51
stress 12, 20-21, 30, 41, 48, 51
suicide 12, 21, 25, 29, 39, 41, 53, 55, 60

tennis 44-45
Tesla, Nikola 26-27
therapists 21, 31, 45, 60
therapy 35, 60
Thunberg, Greta 56-57
transgender 54-55
trauma 6, 9, 19, 20, 55, 59, 61

Vaid-Menon, Alok 54-55
Van Gogh, Vincent 24-25

websites 61
wellbeing 13, 19, 21, 23, 37, 53
Williams, Serena 44-45

yoga 61

For my younger self and every young person in the world—you are not alone
and your mental health matters—RD

You are human before anything else. So be gentle with yourself—IM

Brimming with creative inspiration, how-to
projects, and useful information to enrich your
everyday life, quarto.com is a favourite destination
for those pursuing their interests and passions.

A Mind Like Mine © 2022 Quarto Publishing plc.
Text © 2022 Rachael Davis. Illustrations © 2022 Islenia Mil
First Published in 2022 by Frances Lincoln Children's Books,
an imprint of The Quarto Group.
100 Cummings Center, Suite 265D
Beverly, MA 01915, USA.
T (978) 282-9590 F (978) 283-2742
www.quarto.com

A catalogue record for this book is available from the British Library.

ISBN 978-0-7112-7401-3

The illustrations were created digitally
Set in Burford Base and Brandon Grotesque
Published by Georgia Amson-Bradshaw and Katie Cotton
Designed by Sasha Moxon
Edited by Claire Grace
Production by Dawn Cameron

Manufactured in Guangdong, China TT042022

9 8 7 6 5 4 3 2 1

This book has used the following sources for quotations: *Psychological States and the Artist*, J. Kromm; *The Letters of Michelangelo*, E. H. Ramsden; *Isaac Newton*, A. Storr; *Hans Christian Andersen: The Life of a Storyteller*, J. Wullschlager; *Life And Letters of Charles Darwin*; *Notes on Nursing*, F. Nightingale; www.nobelprize.org; *Health Problems of Alfred Nobel*, S. Sri Kantha; www.vangoghletters.org; *Wizard: The Life and Times of Nikola Tesla*, M. Seifer; *Madame Curie: A Biography*, N. Angier, E. Curie; *A Brilliant Madness*, PBS American Experience documentary; *Magnificent Desolation*, B. Aldrin; *The David Chang Show*, episode 8; *Eat a Peach*, D. Chang; *Living with Bulimia*, BBC documentary, F. Flintoff; *My Life: Queen of the Court*, S. Williams; *Beyond the Gender Binary*, A. Vaid Menon; *Our House is on Fire*, E. Thunberg; *4D with Demi Lovato*, A. Vaid Menon; MIND HK Awards 2020; 2020 Crystal award; www.thelivelovelaughfoundation.org; *Stylist*, J. Jamil.